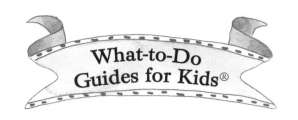

What to Do When

Fear interferes

A Kid's Guide to Overcoming Phobias

by Claire A. B. Freeland, PhD
and Jacqueline B. Toner, PhD

illustrated by Janet McDonnell

MAGINATION PRESS • WASHINGTON, DC
AMERICAN PSYCHOLOGICAL ASSOCIATION

Magination Press
★ Books for Kids from the
American Psychological Association

Magination Press is a registered trademark of the American Psychological Association.
Order books at maginationpress.org, or call 1-800-374-2721.

Book design by Sandra Kimbell
Printed by Worzalla, Stevens Point, WI

Library of Congress Cataloging-in-Publication Data

Names: Freeland, Claire A. B., author. | Toner, Jacqueline B., author. | McDonnell, Janet, illustrator.
Title: What to do when fear interferes : a kid's guide to overcoming phobias / by Claire A. B. Freeland, PhD and Jacqueline B. Toner, PhD ; illustrated by Janet McDonnell.
Description: Washington, DC : Magination Press, [2019] | Series: What-to-do guides for kids | Audience: Age: 6-12.
Identifiers: LCCN 2018035826| ISBN 9781433829741 (pbk.) | ISBN 1433829746 (pbk.)
Subjects: LCSH: Fear in children--Juvenile literature. | Fear--Juvenile literature.
Classification: LCC BF723.F4 F74 2019 | DDC 155.4/1246--dc23 LC record available at https://lccn.loc.gov/2018035826

Manufactured in the United States of America
10 9 8 7 6 5 4 3 2

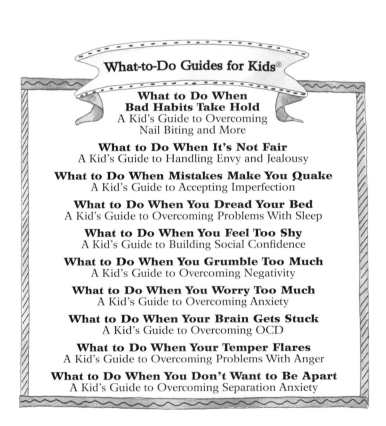

What-to-Do Guides for Kids®

**What to Do When
Bad Habits Take Hold**
A Kid's Guide to Overcoming
Nail Biting and More

What to Do When It's Not Fair
A Kid's Guide to Handling Envy and Jealousy

What to Do When Mistakes Make You Quake
A Kid's Guide to Accepting Imperfection

What to Do When You Dread Your Bed
A Kid's Guide to Overcoming Problems With Sleep

What to Do When You Feel Too Shy
A Kid's Guide to Building Social Confidence

What to Do When You Grumble Too Much
A Kid's Guide to Overcoming Negativity

What to Do When You Worry Too Much
A Kid's Guide to Overcoming Anxiety

What to Do When Your Brain Gets Stuck
A Kid's Guide to Overcoming OCD

What to Do When Your Temper Flares
A Kid's Guide to Overcoming Problems With Anger

What to Do When You Don't Want to Be Apart
A Kid's Guide to Overcoming Separation Anxiety

CONTENTS

Introduction to Parents and Caregivers

A child with a phobia about elevators, heights, or vehicles may demand that adults take the stairs with them to visit a high floor of a building, cower far from the edge of a vista overlook, or cry when asked to sit in the car during rush hour. Phobias about medical procedures, such as injections or fears of seeing blood, can make routine doctor appointments exceedingly challenging.

If your child has such intense fears, you know that it does little good to tell them that there's nothing to be afraid of. Pointing out that a high bridge has a sturdy guard rail will not result in their now feeling comfortable to walk across it. Phobias are by definition irrational. That is, while the person experiencing them may be having physical and emotional reactions similar to ones they would have in the face of imminent danger, the situation they are in doesn't present an actual significant threat. So, reassurance of safety does very little to assuage their fears or to convince them to proceed normally with activities that trigger the phobia.

The approach presented in this book will work most effectively with the help of a parent or other adult "coach." An adult with their own intense fear reactions may find it particularly hard to guide a child in overcoming a fear. If this is the case for you, note that the same process presented in this book can work to lessen your own fears. Don't hesitate to enlist the help of your pediatrician or a mental health professional for support or further guidance.

The most effective way to overcome a phobia is exposure, which requires the child to experience the feared object for a period of time long enough for their extreme physical and emotional reactions to dissipate. One of the greatest challenges in helping a child overcome a phobia can be convincing them to hang in there rather than avoid their fear, and to provide support as they do so. It's important to approach the trigger in a modulated way. Initially, you may need to help your child choose tasks that are far removed from the feared experience, such as imagining a thunderstorm or looking at pictures of insects. Taking it slowly and letting your child experience success by overcoming mildly frightening versions of scary situations will allow them to build confidence in facing increasingly more feared situations.

Phobias can result from frightening or traumatic experiences but, more often, they don't have a known source. Children who tend to be anxious may be particularly likely to develop a specific phobia. You might find other books in the **What-to-do Guides for Kids** series helpful to address related emotional challenges.

Children are particularly susceptible to developing vicarious fears. This happens when they observe another person reacting with intense fear. Or, a fear can develop vicariously by watching a movie where another is afraid or even from a news report that accentuates the damage caused by a storm or the abundance of a particular illness this season.

As you help your child gradually face feared experiences, be cognizant of messages in their world that may serve to reinforce their fears. Gently redirect adult conversation about impending weather events, recent accidents, or out-of-control animals. Judiciously monitor your child's experiences with frightening messages they receive through the media. When such messages permeate your best defenses, counter them with more realistic views of possible danger and how they will stay safe.

By developing positive self-talk, your child can learn to focus on rational thinking and self-cheerleading to encourage themselves to proceed with exposure experiences. Providing rewards, both tangible and social, will help them to feel accomplishment and pride in taking on gradually more difficult challenges. Learning coping strategies that help them to relax and de-stress can reduce overall anxious tendencies, making success more likely.

This book can help you guide your child through the process of overcoming a phobia in a gentle but systematic way. Remember to take it slowly. Work through a chapter or two at a time and encourage your child to do the exercises provided. If your child is hesitant about facing fears, help them to choose experiences to start

with that are not very threatening. As they progress, you will both be surprised that challenges that at first seemed insurmountable will diminish in intensity. And, learning to overcome their fears can result in more freedom to engage in activities and with others with greater self-assurance. Watch your child soar to new heights of confidence!

CHAPTER ONE

Emergencies and False Alarms

Astronauts fly to outer space. They have many different jobs. Some fly the spacecraft. Some orbit the earth or work in a space station or walk on the moon. They might bring supplies to the space station or do science experiments. If they leave their shuttle or space station, they wear special space suits because there is no air in space. When they are in the space station, they float because there is no gravity to keep them on the floor. Astronauts train for years to do their jobs well. There is also a huge team of people on Earth who use computers to help guide their work and keep them safe.

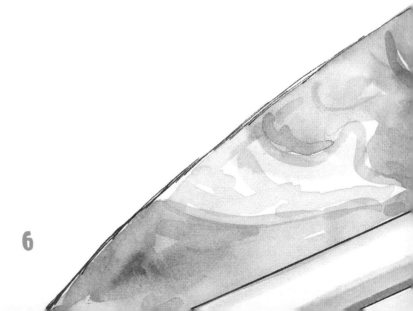

Imagine going into space! What is it like to be weightless and float through the air? What parts of space would you want to explore?

Draw or write about interesting things to experience in space.

One of the reasons that astronauts spend so much time preparing for space travel is that they have to be ready for anything. Space travel is very complicated and emergencies are possible. A space shuttle has all kinds of alarms and flashing lights to alert the crew to any problem that needs attention right away. Astronauts are generally very brave, but if something goes wrong, it can feel quite scary.

Our bodies also send out alarm signals when something happens that could be a problem. What are the signals in our bodies that tell us there's something scary going on? When astronauts face emergencies, their hearts may race. Their faces may get red and their breathing may speed up. They are super focused and working with the team to solve the problem.

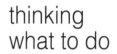

thinking
what to do

face red

heart racing

breathing fast

In an emergency, you would probably respond in a similar way: Your heart may beat faster, you might feel out of breath, and your body may shake. You may feel afraid. It is actually helpful to feel afraid in an emergency. These reactions tell you that you need to take action to avoid danger.

Circle what you feel when you are afraid.

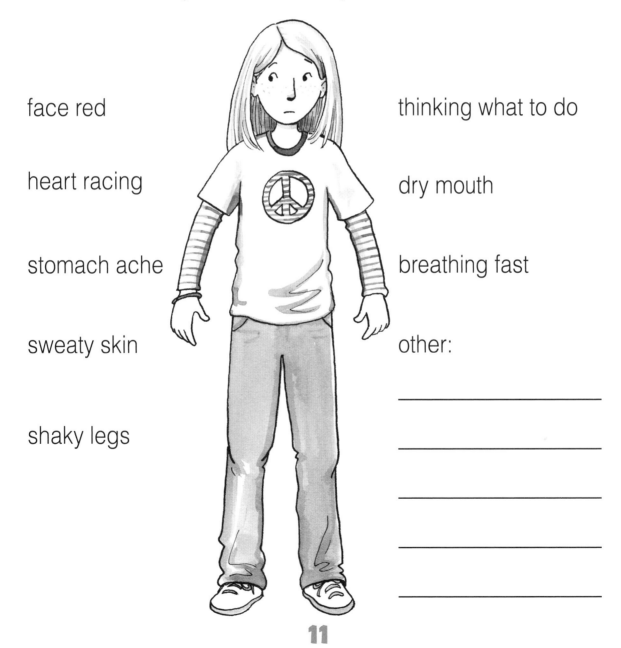

face red

heart racing

stomach ache

sweaty skin

shaky legs

thinking what to do

dry mouth

breathing fast

other:

_____

_____

_____

_____

_____

All kids have fears. It's normal to be afraid, not just in an emergency, but sometimes in everyday life. There are plenty of scary things and scary places. For example, a very loud noise will probably make you jump and feel afraid. Your body is telling you: "Find out what that is! Make sure you're safe!" With everyday fears, we become afraid and then, when we see we're safe, we're over it.

But sometimes kids keep feeling as if there is an emergency when there isn't one. Your body and mind can fool you. Your heart may race or your face may get red or you may start breathing fast. Even though there is not an actual emergency, there is something you are afraid of**...very afraid of...WAY TOO AFRAID OF.** It is important to pay attention to the differences between real emergencies and **false alarms.**

If an alarm on the space station is signaling that the heat shield has been damaged, an astronaut needs to act quickly and alert everyone to begin an emergency response. His ship and those aboard may be in great danger. But it would be a problem if he reacted in the same way to an alarm that was reminding him to water the plants in an onboard science experiment! He might act in a way that is too extreme for the situation.

It's important that an astronaut be able to tell the difference between a real emergency and something that's an everyday experience.

The same is true of you. You need your body to react one way to emergencies and another way to everyday experiences. When the smoke alarm in your house goes off when your parents are cooking, it can be loud and startling, but it doesn't mean there's an emergency. The smoke alarm is letting you know there's more smoke than usual. You might need to put on a fan, but it's not time to call the fire department.

Let's practice noticing the differences between true emergencies and false alarms.

Look at these drawings.

Circle the alarms that signal an emergency.

Put an X on the alarms that you should react to but are not emergencies.

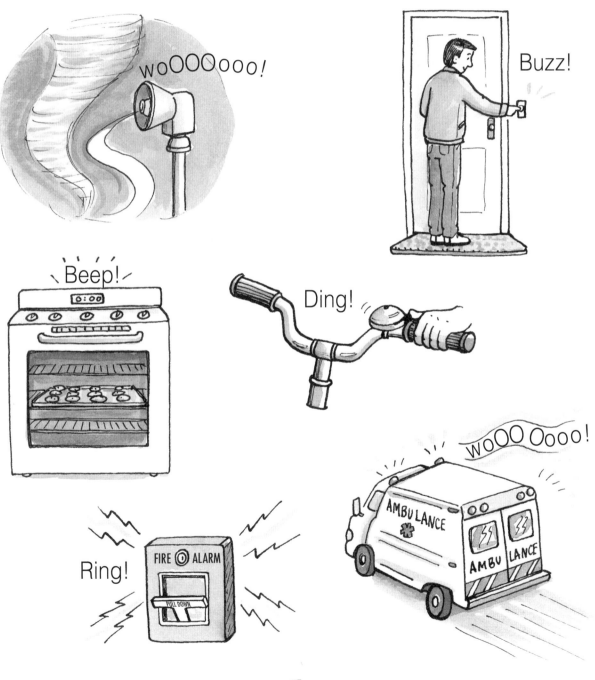

When something that isn't an emergency leads you to feel or think that there is one, and it happens over and over again, we call it a **Phobia.**

A **Phobia** is an unreasonable fear of something. And the fear happens every time you see or experience the something (or maybe even think about the something). The fear is strong and, just like in an emergency, you feel that you have to get away. But, with a phobia, your body is sending out an alarm when you are not in real danger.

You might wonder why you have a phobia. Well, you might have a body that reacts too quickly and too strongly and fools you into thinking there's a danger. Or you might have a body that doesn't recover easily when something scares you. Or, maybe you have had a bad experience that has left you too afraid. Or maybe people in your family have a lot of fears and you've learned from them. Or maybe your mind tends to jump to the worst that could happen. But, most of the time, no one knows how or why a phobia develops. The important thing is that it's not anyone's fault.

Phobias make you feel terrible **and** they can get in the way of doing fun activities and going places you need to go. Phobias just feel too scary!

There are many common phobias. Most people get a little bit nervous around bees, but if you have a phobia, you might run in the house at the first bee sighting. That would be too much of a reaction to a small likelihood of being stung.

It's okay to still have some concern about bees and to take precautions (like wearing shoes outside and staying still if a bee flies too near), but the key is to enjoy playing outside.

Phobias about snakes, storms, lightning, or tornadoes can also make kids afraid to be outside, even in good weather. And that might mean missing picnics, sports games, or outdoor time with friends.

Other kinds of phobias include fears of getting your injections at the doctor, seeing someone hurt, or seeing blood. These kinds of phobias can cause problems if you get very upset when it's time to go to the doctor, or if you say you're not going to school.

And many kids have big fears of dogs or other animals, rollercoasters, clowns, or even balloons. These kinds of phobias may keep you from enjoying visits to friends' houses, school events, or birthday parties.

Phobias of riding in an elevator, flying in a plane, driving over bridges, or being high up can be troublesome and frustrating when going somewhere.

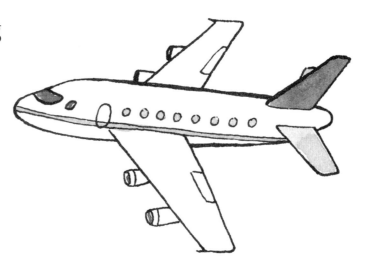

Phobias of the dark and other nighttime fears can make it hard for some kids to settle down at night. Sometimes this can make bedtime take way too long and make it hard to fall asleep until way too late.

Do you have a phobia? Write down what you are too afraid of and how your phobia gets in your way. What problems do your fears cause? Here are two examples.

Phobia	How my phobia interferes
I'm afraid of balloons.	I refuse to go to most birthday parties.
I'm afraid of spiders.	I'm too nervous to go to the playground because there are usually spiders there.

Some kids will have a short list—maybe only one thing! Other kids might have a longer list. No matter how long or short your list, notice the problems your fears are causing you and your family. It can sometimes feel like your fears have taken over.

The good news is that there are ways to keep your phobia from interfering. This book will teach you how. You will learn how to turn off those alarms and flashing lights when you don't need them. No more missing out on all the fun. Watch your confidence soar!

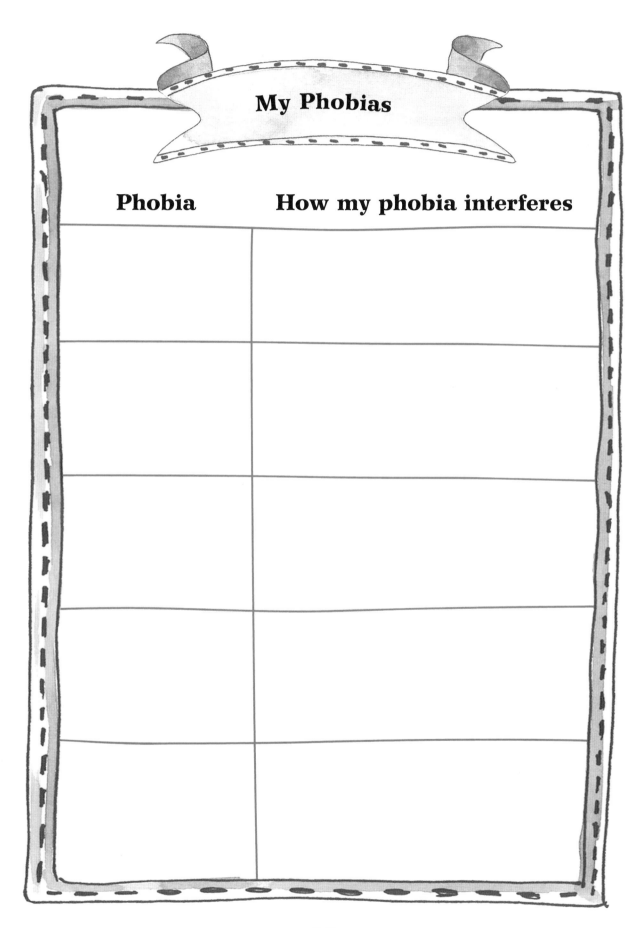

My Phobias

Phobia	How my phobia interferes

23

CHAPTER TWO

Getting Used To It

It takes time and experience to get used to something. When Henry first served on the International Space Station, he found the flashing alarm lights and beeps on the instrument panel upsetting and confusing. Now he is used to them and he knows what to do to take care of problems.

When Audrey first became an astronaut in training, her teachers set up fake emergency situations to see how she would respond.

The sirens made her worried and uncomfortable, but she learned what to do. Now she is ready to perform in space.

Henry and Audrey got used to alarms, sirens, and flashing lights so that they could respond to them, fix problems, and do their jobs well.

Getting used to it. What does it mean? It means that something that used to get our attention a lot no longer does. Let's think of things you might have gotten used to.

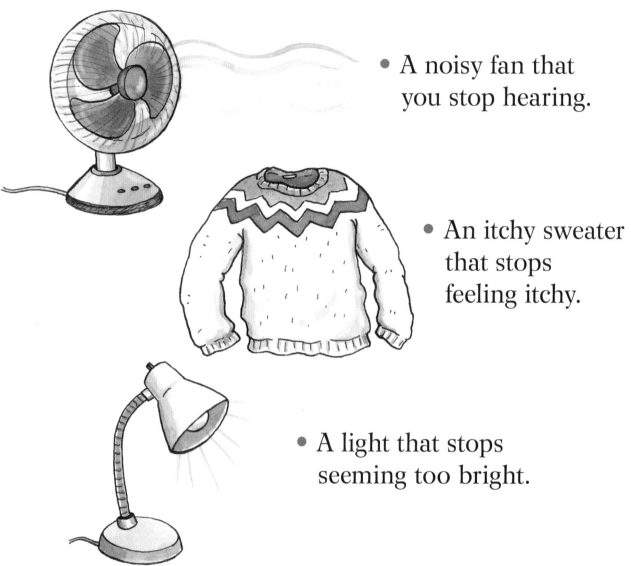

- A noisy fan that you stop hearing.

- An itchy sweater that stops feeling itchy.

- A light that stops seeming too bright.

We are lucky that our bodies are made to get used to things. It would be impossible to learn, play, or listen to a story if we were paying attention to all the sights, sounds, and sensations around us at all times.

You have lots of experience with getting used to new things or changes. Can you list some examples? Think of little things, like sleeping with a new pillow, or wearing a new pair of sneakers!

_____

_____

_____

_____

_____

_____

_____

Of course, it takes time for our bodies to stop reacting. When we avoid something we're afraid of, our bodies don't have the opportunity to adjust. If we keep avoiding what we're afraid of, our fears grow. That's why it's important to **face your fears.** Staying in a safe but scary situation for a while gives our bodies time to get used to it.

Facing our fears is called **exposure.**

Amanda is afraid the swimming pool will be too cold. She sticks her foot in and pulls it back out. She does not let her body get used to the water. Her friend, Tomás, quickly lowers himself into the water. He feels cold, but, after a while, he gets used to the water and has fun at the pool. Tomás's **exposure** to the pool water worked!

Tomás has an idea. He suggests to Amanda that she sit on the side of the pool and let her legs dangle in the water. He understands that she is not ready to get all the way in, but he knows that some **exposure** will help. Sure enough, after a time, Amanda is ready to come in up to her waist. Finally, Amanda and Tomás are able to play together in the pool.

Exposure can come in different forms. Tomás got in right away. Amanda took more time and got in little by little. Both are okay because both lead to getting used to something.

Lucy has always slept with a nightlight. Now her parents are helping her get used to sleeping in a dark room. At first Lucy is feeling unsure as to whether she will be comfortable without a nightlight even though she knows she is safe. Lucy's parents start by leaving on the hall light so she can get used to having less light in her room. After a few nights, they leave on only the bathroom light. Soon Lucy is able to sleep with just a dim nightlight in the bathroom. That gradual **exposure** helped her to get used to a darker room.

Think of one of the things you listed earlier that you got used to. What was that like?

Draw or write about yourself getting used to something.

But the idea that you can overcome your phobias by getting used to the very things that make you so afraid might seem impossible to you right now.

If you are starting to worry that you will have to do things you are not ready for, let us reassure you. We will be asking you to take small enough steps that you feel ready but not so small that you stay stuck with fears that interfere in your life.

Right now all you have to do is turn the page!

CHAPTER THREE

Gauges and Ladders

Owen dreamed of being an astronaut like the ones he had seen in the movies. But Owen had doubts about whether or not he could handle it. He knew he would have to learn a lot of math and science. He also knew that being an astronaut requires great physical fitness and would be very challenging. And, he knew that it was dangerous work. He felt so overwhelmed that he considered giving up on his dream.

But Owen decided that he could start by taking steps towards his goal. He studied hard in school and learned a lot about outer space and engineering. He was excited by how interesting these subjects were.

He exercised every day and gradually got stronger. He went on camping trips and went rock climbing to get used to pushing himself to new levels of fitness. He joined the Air Force and learned to fly planes, got used to heights and moving through space, and even had a few moments of feeling weightless.

After all his hard work, Owen was accepted into the astronaut training program. He felt nervous about the challenges ahead but he knew he could do it by taking one step at a time.

Conquering phobias through **exposure** is also best one step at a time. Just as Owen wasn't ready to be an astronaut when he first dreamed of it, you might not feel ready to take on your scariest fears right away.

In order to figure out the steps that are right for you, plan how you could do a little bit of what you are afraid of without feeling too overwhelmed. You will probably want a grown-up to help you plan your steps.

Write down some scary, not-so-scary, and in-between-scary actions relating to your phobia.

Here is an example for a **dog phobia:**

- Look at dog pictures in a book or on the internet.

- Pet a friend's large dog who is not on a leash.

- Look at a cartoon picture of a dog.

- Watch a video or recording of a large dog growling and barking.

- Watch people walking their dogs, through a window or from far away.

- Sit next to a small dog on a leash.

- Think about a little dog.

- Walk in a park where there are lots of dogs.

- Play with a friend's small dog.

- Sit next to a medium-sized dog on a leash.

Be sure you have some hard steps and some easy steps. Small differences can make your steps easier or harder, so be sure to be very specific.

Here are some tips:

Do the action for more or less time. For example, be near a dog for 5 seconds, 30 seconds, one minute. You've got three steps right there.

Do the action with or without someone. For example, have your parent go with you to visit a friend who has a dog, play with your friend and their dog, play alone with your friend's dog.

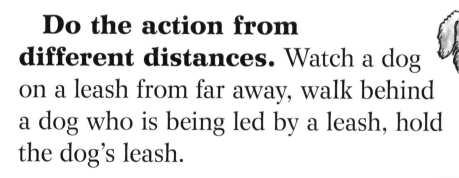

Do the action from different distances. Watch a dog on a leash from far away, walk behind a dog who is being led by a leash, hold the dog's leash.

Do the action using different formats like your imagination, pictures, or videos. Imagine petting a large dog, look at pictures of different kinds of dogs, watch videos of dogs doing different activities.

Before you put your steps in order, check out this fear gauge:

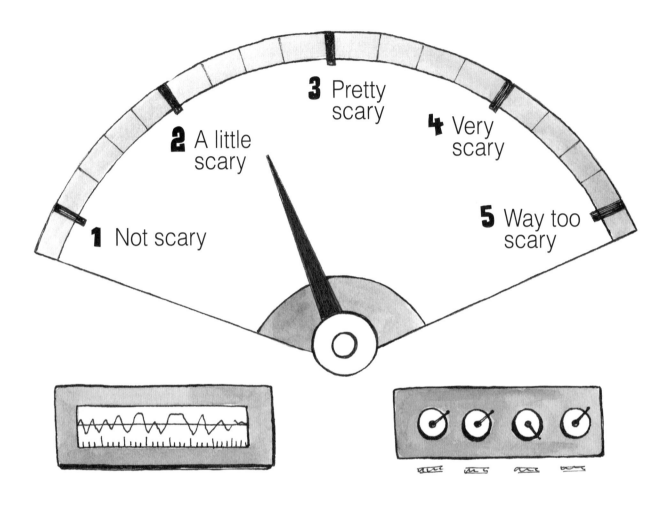

You are using the fear gauge to tell how scared you are of each of the actions you wrote down related to your phobia. Then you'll put your actions in order on a fear ladder. You'll write the scariest actions on the top steps of the ladder. Remember, no one else can tell you how you feel. It's okay if more than one action has the same fear level.

This is what it might look like with the **dog phobia** list above:

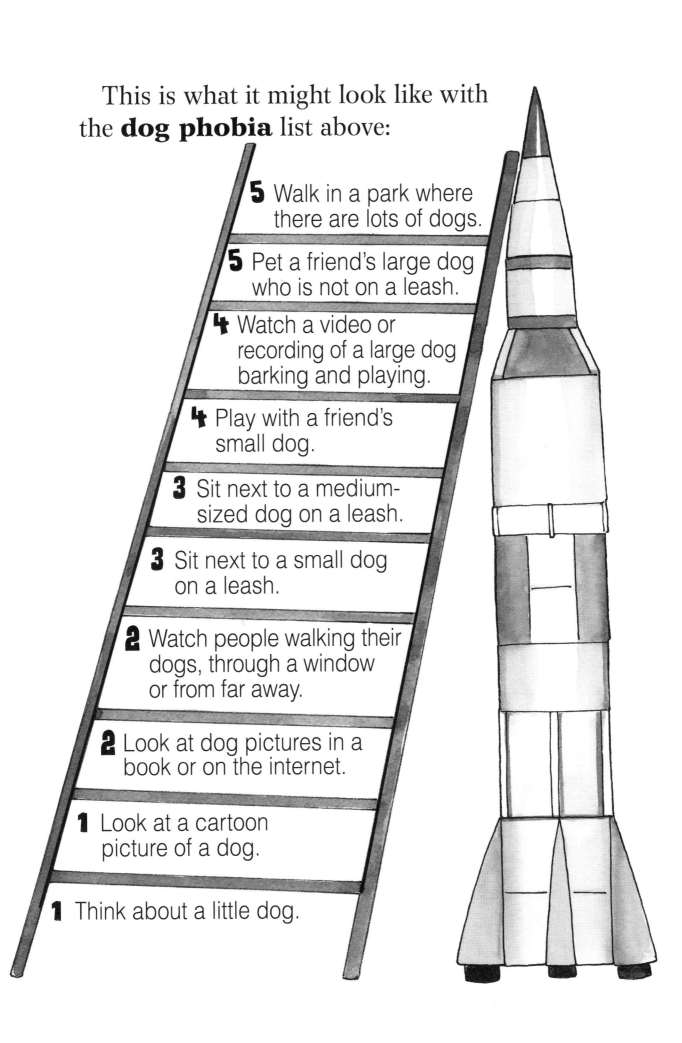

5 Walk in a park where there are lots of dogs.

5 Pet a friend's large dog who is not on a leash.

4 Watch a video or recording of a large dog barking and playing.

4 Play with a friend's small dog.

3 Sit next to a medium-sized dog on a leash.

3 Sit next to a small dog on a leash.

2 Watch people walking their dogs, through a window or from far away.

2 Look at dog pictures in a book or on the internet.

1 Look at a cartoon picture of a dog.

1 Think about a little dog.

Here are some more examples of a few steps for different fears. It's best to have more than one action for each fear rating—we just want to give you some ideas of how to create steps. When you create your own steps, make as many as you need. Be sure you have enough easier ones so you don't rush into something you don't feel ready for.

Phobia of riding in elevators

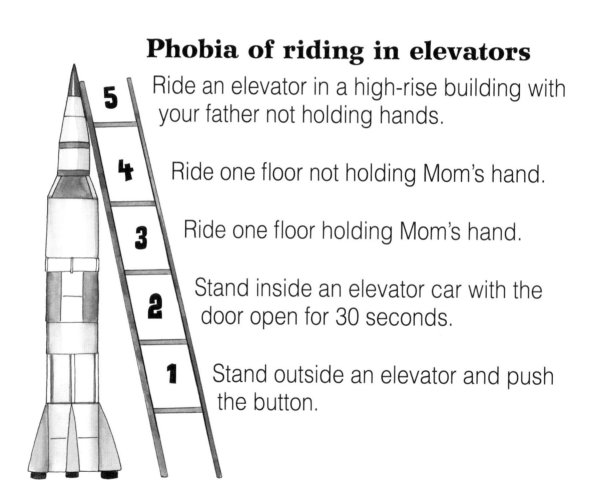

5 Ride an elevator in a high-rise building with your father not holding hands.

4 Ride one floor not holding Mom's hand.

3 Ride one floor holding Mom's hand.

2 Stand inside an elevator car with the door open for 30 seconds.

1 Stand outside an elevator and push the button.

Phobia of getting an injection

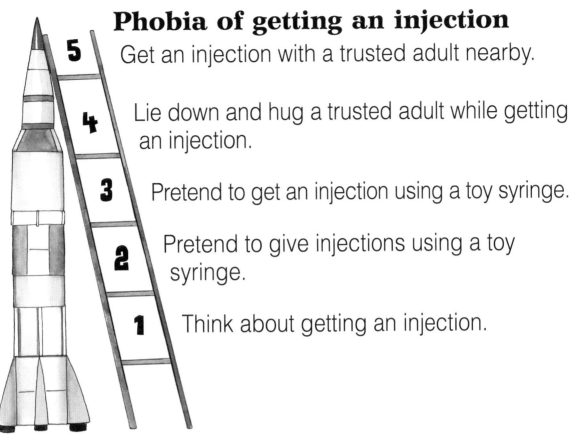

5 — Get an injection with a trusted adult nearby.

4 — Lie down and hug a trusted adult while getting an injection.

3 — Pretend to get an injection using a toy syringe.

2 — Pretend to give injections using a toy syringe.

1 — Think about getting an injection.

Phobia of storms

5 — Watch a storm from a window.

4 — Do an activity during a storm without actually looking outside.

3 — Watch videos of storms with the lights off while someone turns a flashlight on and off.

2 — Read about storms in picture books.

1 — Look out the window on a nice day and see if there are any clouds in the sky.

Now put your list of scary actions here. You are getting ready to blast off for a successful launch to no more phobia!

1 Not scary **2** A little scary **3** Pretty scary
4 Very scary **5** Way too scary

Scary Actions	Gauge
_____	_____
_____	_____
_____	_____
_____	_____
_____	_____
_____	_____
_____	_____
_____	_____
_____	_____

Now put your actions in order on the ladder.

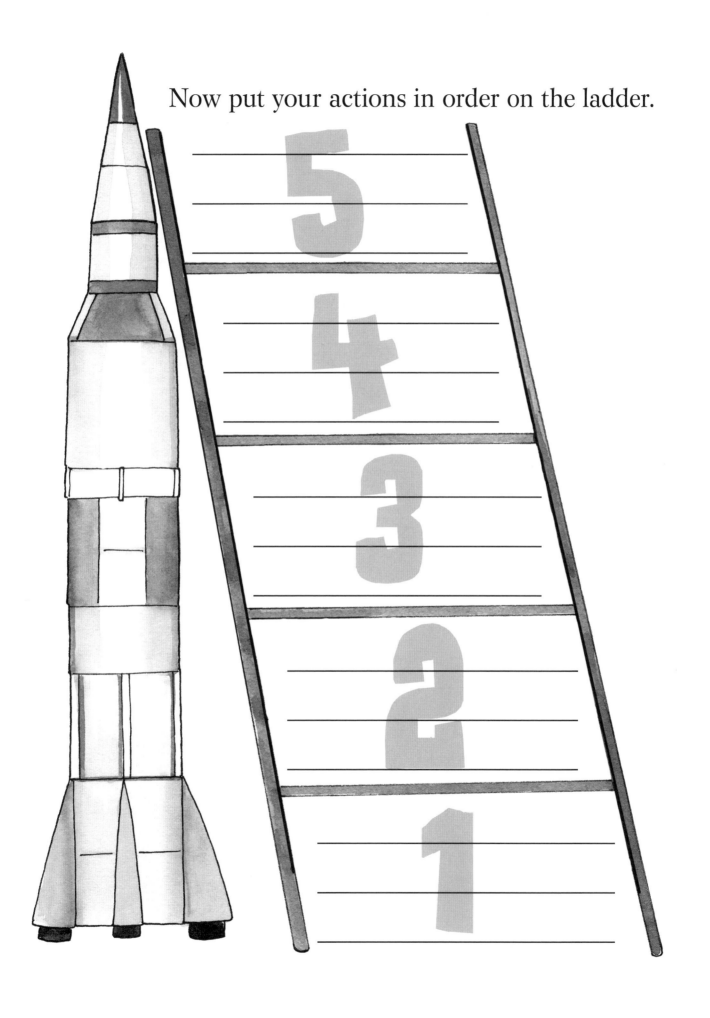

Plan for Obstacles

Astronauts are daring. Their job is to go to places and do things that are tough. They need to be brave! They also need to know how to deal with obstacles they may encounter along the way. There are objects in space, such as parts of old satellites, that may hit the space ship. Or they may have heat shields that need attention. These obstacles could cause serious problems that astronauts have to deal with to stay on course.

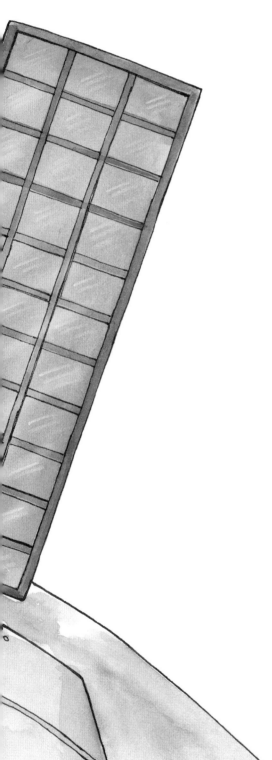

Just like a well-prepared astronaut, you've thought through a variety of actions and how scary they feel for you. You put them in order from least scary to most scary and you've come up with a plan. Once it's time to blast off, you'll start at the bottom of the ladder with the easiest steps. But, just as unexpected obstacles sometimes get in an astronaut's way, you might encounter difficulties in your way, too.

Here are some difficulties that lots of kids have and a few suggestions that will help you make changes to your plan so that you can keep climbing your ladder.

Obstacle: You're too busy thinking about a future step to get used to the current step.

Casper is working on a phobia of flying on an airplane. He's gone through the easiest steps of looking at pictures and videos of airplanes, and his

next step is to go to the airport with his dad and watch the planes. When they arrive at the airport, Casper starts to get upset. He's so busy thinking about having to get on a plane someday that he's hardly paying attention to what's around him!

Let's help Casper with this obstacle.

We can remind Casper to stay **focused** on the step he is facing right now. Casper is worrying about something scary happening in the future. He is working his way up to actually flying on a plane someday, but he's not there yet. He needs a reminder that he is working up to harder steps and that he will be ready when he gets to them. Most of the time, fears on later steps won't be as strong as you imagine they will be. Casper may discover that once he's gotten used to less challenging steps, he'll feel more confident about taking on the higher steps on his ladder. So for now, he needs to **stay focused!** His success will lead to more success!

Obstacle: You keep asking your parent or other adult to tell you that you are okay, that you are safe.

At the airport, Casper clings to his dad and asks him lots of questions about the dangers of air travel. Casper and his dad have talked about how answering those kinds of questions will help him feel better in the short run, but in the long run the reassurance of those answers gets in the way of going ahead and facing fears. Having a parent nearby might be a part of your steps, but remind yourself to **stay strong** and take each step with **no questions.**

Obstacle: As you blast off, you may find that the steps on your ladder are out of order, or that the next step is too big.

If that happens, you can make some changes in your flight path. You can **re-order** your steps or **add a new step** in between. As long as you take steps, adding some in is okay. Or, maybe you need to **repeat a step** a few times. We all have ups and downs, even astronauts! It doesn't matter how fast you climb that ladder. What counts is that you are moving forward, headed in the right direction, and working on facing your fear.

Maybe Casper could change how fast he's going up the ladder and add an in-between step, like finding a quiet spot in the airport to play cards for a while before he moves on to watching the airplanes taking off.

Obstacle: You continue to feel fearful, even as you move up the ladder.

That's okay! Why? Because when you can go about your day without avoiding situations, and you tolerate your discomfort, then that's success. Sometimes astronauts have to adjust for obstacles, but they know they have to keep soaring. The obstacles may still be there, but if you **stay the course,** great job! In time your fear will lessen or even go away.

Casper is feeling uncomfortable at the airport, but he knows if he adapts his plan and **stays the course,** he can make it through!

Match each obstacle to a possible solution. Some might have more than one possible answer!

Obstacles	Solutions
Keep asking your dad if you'll be okay.	Stay the course
Finished a step on the ladder but still feeling a bit uncomfortable.	Repeat a step
Practiced a step but fear gauge still at 5.	Re-order your steps
Your next step now makes you more afraid than the one after it.	No questions
You feel calm about previous steps but you don't feel ready for the next one.	Stay focused
You keep worrying about how scary the last step on the ladder is.	Add a new step

Khalia has a phobia of spiders. The first step on her ladder is to look at pictures of spiders in a book. That was very easy for her.

The second step is to go down to the basement where she's pretty sure there are some spiders. She bursts into tears at the top of the stairs and her fear gauge is at 5.

Can you think of some in-between steps for Khalia?

5

Go down in the basement where there are spiders.

4

_____

_____

_____

3

_____

_____

2

_____

_____

1

Look at pictures of spiders in a book.

What are some other ways Khalia can adjust her plan to avoid this obstacle?

_____

_____

_____

_____

_____

_____

Remember, if you don't feel like you can move up your ladder, it may mean that you need to adjust your plan. And now you know some ways to do that. Staying focused on the step you are working on with no reassurance questions, adding steps, re-ordering steps, and repeating steps will give you the practice that you need to face your fears. The most important thing is to keep taking steps. Stay the course.

FOCUS

no questions

RE-order
REpeat
ADD

STAY the course

To feel courage and take steps on your ladder, it helps to give yourself a pep talk. What you say to yourself really makes a difference in your feelings and actions. You are used to thinking about your phobia in ways that keep you scared. But you can learn a new way of thinking. Find out how to start your steps with a "full tank."

Filling Your Fuel Tank

A great flight plan and strategies to deal with unexpected problems is very important, but for space travel to succeed, astronauts need to be sure that their rocket ship is prepared before they take off. They will check that their fuel tank is full.

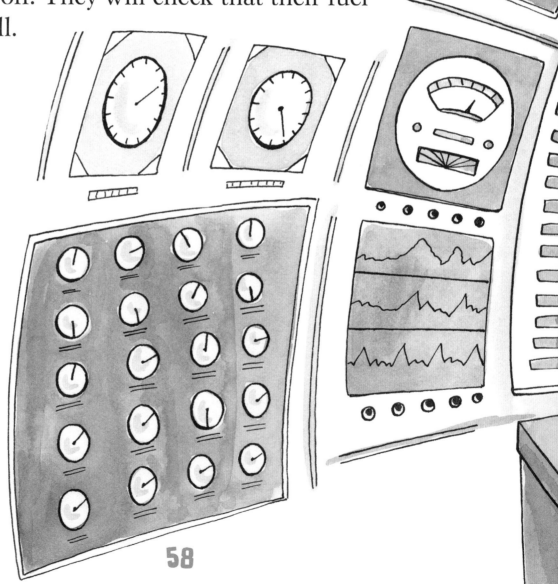

One way in which you can prepare to be successful is to fuel up with new ways of thinking.

When space station alarms and flashing lights go off, they send a message: There's an emergency. An astronaut might have many different thoughts: I need to figure out what's wrong, that heat shield alarm is so loud, those flashing lights remind me of one of our training exercises, and so forth.

You also have thoughts when you are afraid. But many of these thoughts are not helpful and may even make the situation worse:

A snake is going to bite me.

The dentist will hurt me.

I'm going to catch those germs.

I will fall.

As you think about tackling the steps that you wrote in chapter three, you might think:

Thoughts like these are **unhelpful self-talk.** You are telling yourself that you will fail. And, yes, you guessed it: You need **helpful self-talk!**

You need to remind yourself that you are safe and that you are capable.

Let's practice **helpful self-talk.**

The astronauts on the International Space Station work together to use a robotic arm to carry supplies from the space shuttle to the Space Station. Their team work keeps the crew safe. As part of their mission, they created signs with **helpful self-talk.** They thought of some, but they need your help to think of some others. Fill in the empty signs with thoughts that the astronauts can use to feel good and take on the challenges of running the Space Station.

I will **face my fears**

Unhelpful self-talk puts road blocks in your way. Helpful self-talk gets you to your goals.

Try this maze. Take the space shuttle to the space station. Don't let unhelpful self-talk block your path.

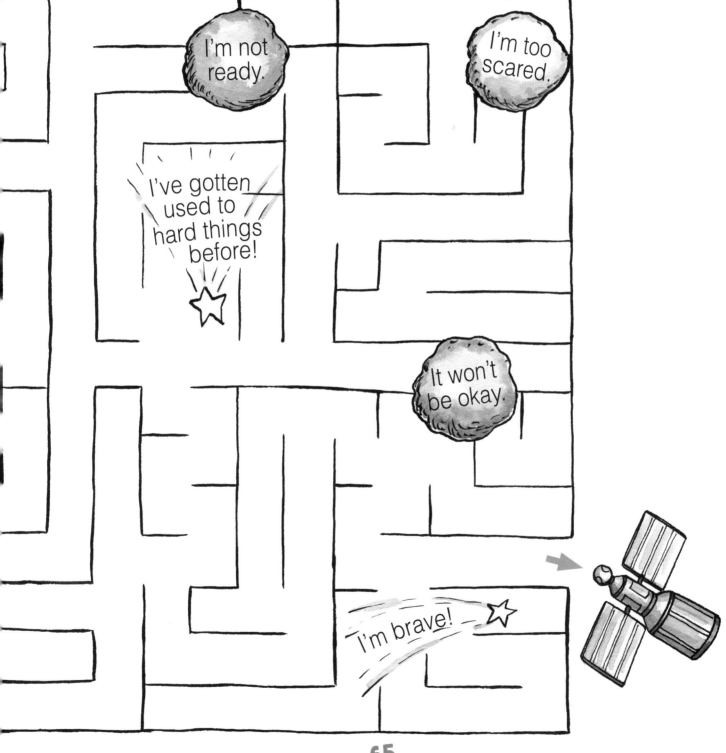

Vanessa wants to overcome her fear of deep water. She has made her ladder of steps to challenge her fears, but some unhelpful self-talk is making it harder.

Help her out by putting a big X on her **UNHELPFUL SELF-TALK** and circling her **helpful self-talk.**

I'll sink.

I'll be proud of myself when I do it.

Playing in the water looks fun!

I can do this!

I'll never be good at this.

This is the scariest thing ever.

Everybody needs **helpful self-talk.** It helps us to feel confident and take on challenges.

There are some other ways that people get inspired to be brave. One is they think about or invent a brave character. This person or character can be your personal space hero.

Draw your space hero
or
cut out and paste here.

Write three worries you have as you get ready to **face your fears**:

_____

_____

_____

Write three things your space hero might whisper in your ear to help you feel confident and brave:

_____

_____

_____

Did your space hero advise you to use **helpful self-talk?** Remind you that your fear is a **false alarm?** Encourage you to slow down and give yourself time to get calmer? Great ideas!

So as you begin your steps to overcome your phobia, practice your **helpful self-talk** and remind yourself of your space hero's advice. Be inspired to **face your fears.** And, as you calm your mind, it will also help to learn how to calm your body and stay in charge of yourself when your alarm bells are ringing.

CHAPTER SIX

Quieting the Alarms

Remember in the first chapter of this book when you learned about all the ways your body may react when the alarm bells are ringing (like your heart pounding, sweating, getting red in the face, feeling short of breath)?

Well, you can feel calmer by learning to control your breathing. Breathing exercises are a really good way to practice relaxing your body.

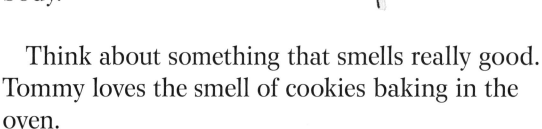

Think about something that smells really good. Tommy loves the smell of cookies baking in the oven.

Gigi thinks the smell of grass that's just been cut is really nice. You can try one of these smells or choose one of your own.

Now, sit or lay down in a comfy place, close your eyes, and as you breathe in, imagine that smell. You can also imagine yourself in a relaxing place (in a hammock, on a beach, floating on a cloud, etc.). After you've taken a big breath in through your nose, blow it out through your mouth slowly. Make sure you get as much air out as you can so you have lots of room to bring in that yummy smell again. Repeat this five times.

Deep smell-breathing not only helps your breathing slow down but also calms your heart, your muscles, your sweat glands, and your brain. It's a good idea to practice deep breathing every day. As you get better at it, it will help you when you begin to feel afraid. When you slow down your breathing, you will stay calmer as you **face your fears.**

After there is an emergency in the space station, the astronauts need to de-stress. It's important that they know how to relax. Of course, an astronaut who just avoided a crisis in space won't be able to "just relax." She may need to do something active to help her body to calm down. Different people find different activities relaxing and it can be helpful to try a lot of different ones to find what works best for you.

John finds it hard to sit quietly after he gets upset. He knows the best way for him to feel calmer is to go shoot hoops. You may also find that physical activity you enjoy will help you relax. It might be shooting baskets, dancing, or climbing in a gym.

When she feels tense, Sophia finds it helpful to be with other people. She knows that if she spends time with friends, bakes cookies with her dad, or plays a game with her mom, she will start to feel more relaxed.

Being creative helps Xander to de-stress. Painting, drawing, and building with interlocking blocks are his favorite ways of calming down.

What are five things you might be able to do to help you relax?

1 _____

2 _____

3 _____

4 _____

5 _____

Being active, being social, and being creative all assist in taking your body and your mind to a calmer place. They direct your body's energy in helpful ways so you can relax before and after you've taken steps on your phobia ladder. Teaching your body to relax will also reduce the chances that your body will send off false alarms at times when you are safe.

You now have the information and skills you need to think in a helpful way, keep your body calm, and take steps on the ladder to conquering your phobia.

CHAPTER SEVEN

Blast Off!

You are ready to blast off. Just like an astronaut who has trained for space travel, you have learned about how to take the steps to be less afraid and keep your phobia from interfering in your life. You will start with the easiest actions, the ones at the bottom of your ladder. Remember to stay in a challenging situation until you get used to it. It's a good idea to do each step twice (or more!) to make sure you really master them. Don't move on to a harder step until the one you're on feels like a 2 or 1 on your fear gauge. If one of your steps includes something that ends very quickly (like an elevator ride) you may have to repeat it right away to give yourself time to get used to it. So, let's get started!

You wrote your steps in chapter three. Now start with the easiest step on your rocket ladder. You may feel uncomfortable at first, but remember that your fear level will go down as you face your fear, your body adjusts, and you get used to the situation. Go ahead and give it a try. Fill in the chart below:

First step on ladder			
Fear gauge at the beginning of practice		Fear gauge at the end of practice	
Obstacles you avoided			

We hope your first step went well. But even if it was really hard, good for you for trying. We think each and every step of the way deserves a reward. It is important to celebrate your effort.

There are many ways to set up rewards. You and a grown up should talk about what will work best for you. We'll give you one suggestion: use the game board on the next page! Fill in the small, medium, and big rewards you and your parent or other grown-up agree to.

Small Rewards

_____

_____

_____

Medium Rewards

_____

_____

_____

Big Rewards

_____

_____

_____

When you complete a step, move around the board (fear gauge 2 – move two spaces; fear gauge 3 – move three spaces and so forth). When you land on a reward space, you earn that reward! You are working hard to **face your fears.** Every time you practice, even if you are repeating a step, move towards another reward.

Remember, you may need to repeat a step before moving on. If you do the first step again, fill in this chart:

First step on ladder (second practice)			
Fear gauge at the beginning of practice		Fear gauge at the end of practice	
Obstacles you avoided			

Was your experience different this time? Were you a little less afraid at the start? Now it's time to decide whether your fear gauge is low enough to start on the next step. If it isn't, repeat the first step again. When your fear gauge starts to come down, you can keep taking steps up the ladder. Don't skip steps, and make sure to keep track of what happens to your fear gauge as you move forward. That will help you see how you are changing with practice and what tools work well for you. Getting through your fear ladder will probably take days or even weeks. No need to rush it! After all, becoming a successful astronaut takes time.

Keep working up your ladder one step at a time and track your progress. You may need a bigger chart than this one, so feel free to continue on another piece of paper.

NEXT step on ladder			
Fear gauge at the beginning of practice		Fear gauge at the end of practice	
Obstacles you avoided			

NEXT step on ladder			
Fear gauge at the beginning of practice		Fear gauge at the end of practice	
Obstacles you avoided			

NEXT step on ladder			
Fear gauge at the beginning of practice		Fear gauge at the end of practice	
Obstacles you avoided			

NEXT step on ladder			
Fear gauge at the beginning of practice		Fear gauge at the end of practice	
Obstacles you avoided			

NEXT step on ladder			
Fear gauge at the beginning of practice		Fear gauge at the end of practice	
Obstacles you avoided			

CHAPTER EIGHT

You Can Do It!

Remember, it's important for your body and mind to set off alarms when you are in danger, but you don't want to have those upsetting feelings at times when you are safe. Phobias can interfere with fun activities and time with friends or make simple activities challenging.

You can get control of false alarms with some smart strategies and practice. Climb up the steps of your fear ladder gradually and notice how your body learns to get used to the different actions. Through the **exposures** you created for your ladder you **face your fears.** As you get used to handling your phobia, your false alarms quiet down. Your practice is really paying off.

Remember:

- The more often you practice, the better. Just like when you practice the piano or soccer, facing fears also requires practice. If you can do a step (or repeat one if you need to) almost every day, that's the best.

- Remind yourself that every step on the ladder is safe. Your fear is tricking you and sending out **false alarms.** With every step you take to beat your phobia, your anxiety gets weaker.

- Let realistic **helpful self-talk** replace alarming thoughts.

- Practice calm breathing.

- De-stress with relaxing activities.

- Believe in yourself!

Facing your fears isn't easy, but by facing the mildly scary ones first, and practicing often, you can shrink your fears down to a more manageable size. Now your fears won't interfere.

Awarded for bravery

in the face of

false alarms to

_____

(name)

Good
★
Job!